Leader's Guide   ᏯᎧᏯᎧᏯᎧᏯᎧᏯᎧᏯᎧᏯᎧᏯᎧᏯᎧ

Guided Meditations for Adults:
Salvation, Joy, Faith, Healing

A QUIET PLACE APART

Leader's Guide ᘓᘐ ᘓᘐ ᘓᘐ ᘓᘐ ᘓᘐ ᘓᘐ ᘓᘐ ᘓᘐ

Guided Meditations for Adults: Salvation, Joy, Faith, Healing

Jane E. Ayer

Saint Mary's Press
Christian Brothers Publications
Winona, Minnesota

The publishing team included Robert P. Stamschror, development editor; Jacqueline M. Captain, manuscript editor; Alan S. Hanson, typesetter; inside illustrations by Elaine Kohner; Stephan Nagel, cover designer; Maurine R. Twait, art director; cover photo by PhotoDisc; pre-press, printing, and binding by the graphics division of Saint Mary's Press.

The acknowledgments continue on page 44.

Printed in the United States of America

Printing: 9 8 7 6 5 4 3 2 1

Year: 2004 03 02 01 00 99 98 97 96

ISBN 0-88489-393-6

 Genuine recycled paper with 10% post-consumer waste. Printed with soy-based ink.

Contents

To my sister, Cheryl,
who has always been like an angel to me
and
to her husband, David,
who is now with the angels,
with loving gratitude
for the many shared experiences of the Holy One.

Directions for Leading the Meditations

As the meditation leader, your preparation is especially important to the success of a guided meditation. Pray the meditation before leading a group in it. This will help you to become comfortable with its style and content. Some material may require a brief doctrinal review with the group. By praying the meditation first, you will become aware if there is a need to do this.

If you choose to have your group do the optional art expression as follow-up to the meditations, it is best if you try it out before the group gathers to make sure it works well and to know better what directions to give.

If you intend to guide the meditations yourself rather than use the accompanying cassette or compact disc, rehearse the guided prayer, including the introductory comments, the scriptural reading, and the opening and closing prayers, so that appropriate and sufficient time is allowed for the imagery to take place and for prayerful reflection to occur. The meditations should be read slowly and prayerfully, using soft instrumental music as a background.

Only a good reader who has prepared should read aloud the scriptural passage that precedes each guided meditation. The scriptural passage is important to establishing the theme and tone of the meditation. Read it with reverence and expression, using a Bible.

PARTICIPANT
PREPARATION To introduce praying a guided meditation, it might be helpful to explain that the participants will be using a prayer form that will call upon their imagination, and that the

Holy Spirit graces our imagination during prayer to help communicate with God. Remember that this type of prayer may not be easy for everyone in the group. Some may be self-conscious about closing their eyes; some may have difficulty getting in touch with their feelings; some may have personal obstacles in their relationship with the Lord. Be gentle, let go, and let the Spirit work. In fact, participants can be told that although the meditation is guided, if the Spirit leads them in another direction, it is okay for them to go with their own reflection and not worry about the words being spoken.

A possible difficulty, one that may not be apparent at first, may be encountered by those who wear the type of contact lenses that prevent them from closing their eyes for an extended period of time. Invite these participants to put their head down, hiding their eyes in the dark crook of their arm, if they are unable to remove the lenses. Another possible difficulty may be experienced by those who have a sinus problem or asthma. Instead of breathing through their nose during the deep-breathing exercises, they can breathe quietly through their mouth.

MUSIC
Quiet music is important for setting and keeping the mood of the meditation. Music can be playing even as the group gathers. It is a nice background for giving instructions. Have additional tapes or compact discs ready to play during the activities after the guided meditation. Ideally, the follow-up activities will take place in a separate space; therefore, it is less disruptive if cassette or CD players are already set up in the different areas.

REFLECTION QUESTIONS
Allowing time for the participants to reflect and name the experience they have just gone through is a necessary part of these prayer experiences. The reflection questions will help the participants do this successfully. Choose several reflection questions (or use questions similar to them) and type them up, leaving room after each for a response. Make a copy for each participant. Allot enough time for each person

to respond to the questions and to share his or her responses with the group. These prayer experiences are not meant to be rushed.

To avoid disrupting the quiet mood of the meditation time, pass out the reflection questions (placed facedown) as the participants take their places. Also give a pen or pencil to each person. If people are sitting on the floor, you could give out hardcover books or clipboards to facilitate writing. Explain that you are distributing reflection questions for use after the meditation.

Assure the participants that their responses are private and that their papers are not going to be collected. When it is time for sharing, honor and affirm all responses, and respect those persons who do not wish to answer aloud.

ART EXPRESSION AND PRAYER RITUAL (OPTIONAL)

Each prayer experience comes with an optional art expression containing a prayer ritual. You might choose to use this rather than the reflection questions.

If you choose to do the optional art expression, prepare the art materials ahead of time and lay them out in the area where the participants will work. Familiarize the group with the art activity before the prayer time, if possible, so as not to disrupt the meditation mood. This should allow you to give particular directions for the art activity without having to answer a lot of questions. If you have previously completed the art expression, it might be helpful to show your sample artwork at this time.

SETTING

It is imperative that the area for the prayer experience is quiet—no ringing of telephones, bells, and the like. If necessary, put a sign on the outside of your door: Praying! Please do not disturb!

Participants may sit in chairs or find a comfortable position on the floor, but they must be a few feet from one another so that they each have their own space and do not distract one another. Therefore, the area must not be cramped. Lying down on the floor should be discouraged, as some participants are likely to fall asleep.

CENTERPIECE

Each theme of the prayer experiences can be enhanced by creating a centerpiece that can be placed on a small table, an altar, or the middle of the floor. The centerpiece should include objects that reflect the message of the prayer. For example, for the meditation on salvation ("Come Down from the Tree"), you might display a tree branch, a loaf of bread, and a bottle of wine. Include candles and a Bible opened to the scriptural passage.

A centerpiece for the meditation on joy ("I Am Chosen, Too!") might include a statue of the Blessed Virgin, candles, and an open Bible.

A centerpiece for the meditation on faith ("Walking on Water") might include a replica or picture of a boat, perhaps in a stormy sea, candles, and an open Bible.

To enhance the meditation on healing ("Time to Unbend"), the centerpiece might consist of a decoratively draped cloth with a cane, a walking stick, or perhaps a pair of open shackles lying on it, candles, and an open Bible.

MATERIALS NEEDED FOR EACH MEDITATION

- a Bible
- an audiotape or CD player
- the meditation recording or script
- tapes or CDs of instrumental music
- reflection questions (a copy for each participant)
- pens or pencils
- clipboards or hardcover books to facilitate writing, if needed
- materials for the art expression (optional; see individual project's needs)
- a centerpiece to reflect the theme (optional)
- a sign that reads Praying! Please do not disturb!

Salvation
Come Down from the Tree

This freeing prayer experience, "Come Down from the Tree," is based on Jesus' gift of salvation given to Zacchaeus when he was called to come down from the sycamore tree. It reminds us that Jesus gives this gift of salvation to each of us despite our sinfulness.

THEME   After you have given directions to the participants and set the tone for meditation, introduce the theme by saying something like the following:

> There is a need to enter into a quiet place if we are to look deeply within ourselves at the scarred areas of our lives that require saving grace. There is a certain amount of readiness necessary on our part if we are to hear the same Lord who called to Zacchaeus and if we are to respond to the same invitation to hurry, come

down, and share at table. We have only to climb down from the tree.

OPENING Read aloud this opening prayer:

> Lord, allow us the gift of quiet so that we may hear you call us. Free us from the trappings and the pain from which we cannot escape without your love. Help us to risk the climb down from the tree, to be open at table, and to accept the salvation you have claimed for us. Amen.

SCRIPTURE Read aloud Luke 19:1–10, using a Bible.

SCRIPT Play the "Come Down from the Tree" meditation on the accompanying recording or slowly and reverently read aloud the following script for the guided meditation. Play soft, instrumental background music.

> Today you will enter the hush of your quiet place and meet Jesus in your imagination. First, you will begin by doing some deep-breathing exercises. If possible, breathe in and out through your nose very quietly during these exercises. Close your eyes and get comfortable. You will be relaxing your entire body.
>
> Breathe in deeply . . . hold it . . . breathe out slowly and completely. Breathe in deeply . . . hold it . . . breathe out slowly and completely. Again, breathe in deeply . . . hold it . . . breathe out slowly and completely.
>
> Allow your feet and ankles to relax. Relax your legs and your hips. Stay mindful of your breathing. Relax your stomach muscles, and now your chest. . . . Just relax. Let your arms grow limp. . . . Relax your wrists, your hands, and your fingers. . . . Keep breathing in deeply and out slowly.

Allow your shoulders to become heavy. . . . Let all the tension drain from your shoulders. . . . Relax your neck, your facial muscles, and even your eyelids. . . . Just relax. . . . Breathe in deeply . . . hold it . . . breathe out slowly and completely. [Pause.]

Today you are on the crowded streets of Jericho. The air is warm, and it is filled with excitement. There is animated chatter all around you. That Jesus of Nazareth is coming! That Jesus whom you have heard so much about. You, too, have a curiosity. You question if Jesus is as wonderful as people say.

As you walk in the midst of hundreds of people, you are continually being jostled and shoved. But you are determined to catch sight of this man, Jesus. You bend over to remove a pebble from your sandal and you are so rudely bumped that you almost lose your balance. . . . You begin to be somewhat annoyed by that and by the fact that you cannot see over the heads of the crowd. You are tired of being harassed, pushed, and disregarded; but despite this irritation, you are unwavering in your resolve. You will find a way to see. . . . You decide to climb a sycamore tree that you spot up ahead. You know that it will give you a decent perch from which to view the approaching Jesus.

You climb the sycamore tree with a little trouble . . . but finally, you settle on one of its gnarled limbs. You are aware that the murmurs from the voices below are growing into shouts. The name of Jesus is beginning to be chanted. Jesus! Jesus! Jesus! All of a sudden, you see an opening in the crowd through which a calm figure walks. It is he. Jesus.

You watch as Jesus stops to place gentle hands in blessing on the head of a woman who is crying. . . . At first you wonder what her problem is, but deep down you wish that those hands were on your head.

The crowd moves forward and with it, Jesus. As he gets closer, you are able to see the fatigue in his face . . . although it doesn't seem to be an issue with him. Jesus stops and speaks and touches and smiles with a compassion that you have never before witnessed. . . . You stretch as far out from your tree limb as you dare because you hope to hear what Jesus is saying. . . . And now, Jesus has stopped just beneath your tree, and he looks directly up at you.

Hear Jesus say your name. . . . Hear Jesus tell you to hurry and come down. . . . There is pleasure in his voice as he tells you that he is going to eat at your house tonight. . . . Notice what you are feeling when Jesus tells you this. . . .

Because of your feelings, it takes you longer to climb out of the tree and to reach the ground. . . . Hear yourself tell Jesus that you are not sure what you have in the cupboards to fix for supper. . . . His voice is warm as he assures you that it is not for the food that he is coming to visit. . . . You believe Jesus. You try not to worry about supper.

The two of you begin to walk down the street. . . . You cannot help but hear the grumblings of your neighbors and the strangers in the crowd. They are reminding Jesus that you are a sinner. . . . They are letting Jesus know how shocked they are that he should want to eat with a sinner. They ask Jesus if he knows what you have done. . . . Jesus only smiles at them.

There is a growing desire in your heart to tell Jesus the areas in your life that you are not proud of. . . . You realize that it is not because of the crowd's gossip that you will confess your pain and guilt but, rather, it is because of the genuine effect that Jesus is having on you.

You have reached your house, and Jesus stops deliberately. He looks into your eyes. Hear Jesus announce that salvation has come to your house today! . . . Without hesitation, he turns and looks squarely at the crowd—at the people who have accused you. Jesus is giving you a gift. He is standing in support of you. You are humbled by this. There is a warmth that floods through you. . . . Allow yourself to feel the warmth that Jesus offers. . . . And yet, there is much you know that you want to unburden.

You enter your home and invite Jesus to come and eat. As Jesus sits at your table, on which you have now placed a loaf of bread and a bottle of wine, you are aware that he looks so comfortable being there with you.

You sense it is time to share what has kept you from getting nearer to Jesus. You share those things that have hardened your heart. You share those people whom you have not loved faithfully or generously. You share those things that you have regrettably not done. You share the fears that paralyze you. Take this time to talk and notice how intently Jesus leans toward you to hear your words and to respond to them.

Hear Jesus once more tell you that you are saved. . . . Listen as he assures you that his presence and peace are with you always to provide you with the graces needed to win over the dark areas of your life.

It is time for Jesus to leave. Tell Jesus how you are feeling as you walk him to the door. . . . At the door, Jesus places both his hands in blessing upon your head. . . . Listen to his prayer for you. . . . You know that this is how that woman in the crowd must have felt. Hear Jesus say your name and that he loves you.

Jesus leaves your doorstep but turns one more time and looks at you with love. You know that you shall never forget this experience or the conversation you had with him. As you watch Jesus walk away, you vow that this time together will make a difference in your life . . . for you will remember that you heard the words that you are saved . . . that you are loved!

Breathe in deeply . . . hold it . . . breathe out slowly and completely. Breathe in deeply . . . hold it . . . breathe out slowly and completely. Once more, breathe in deeply . . . hold it . . . breathe out slowly and completely. And when you are ready, you may open your eyes.

REFLECTION Continue to play instrumental music. Ask the participants to reflect on the experience that they have just gone through by pondering some of the following questions. You might want to suggest that they respond to those questions that speak most to them. Allow time for them to write their reflections.

- What was my initial reaction to being in the midst of a crowd on a hot day?
- What were my thoughts as I watched Jesus move through the throngs of people?
- What feelings did I experience when Jesus stopped beneath my tree and extended his invitation to come down and take him home with me?
- What did I hear the crowd mumbling about me? Were people there that I knew?

- What affect did their gossip have on me? Did Jesus' presence make a difference?
- How did I feel when Jesus said that salvation had come to my house today?
- What were the fears, relationships, or burdens that I shared with Jesus? What was Jesus' response to me about them?
- What is a positive, concrete action that I will choose as a result of my time with Jesus?
- What was Jesus' prayer for me? Could I feel his hands in blessing upon my head?
- What is the most memorable message or image from this prayer experience?

ART EXPRESSION AND PRAYER RITUAL (OPTIONAL)

The art expression is an optional activity. It can be used in place of the reflection questions. If you decide to use this activity, prepare the art area before the group gathers.

At each place, have crayons or watercolor paints and brushes, white or manila drawing paper, and cups of water and paper toweling (if painting is to be done).

After the meditation, continue playing quiet music in the art area. Invite the participants to move to one of the prepared places. Direct them to fold their art paper in half into a card. On the outside of the card, they are to express through colors, symbols, and words, the invitation that Jesus extended to them, and on the inside they are to express their response to that invitation.

Explain that sharing faith experiences can help strengthen one another's faith. Then invite the participants to share Jesus' invitation to them and their response by explaining their artwork. When they are finished—in a moment of silence—have them lift the open card high as gesture of commitment, and place it in the center of the prayer circle (or any other designated place).

Allow time for the sharing and affirming of each person. Continue playing instrumental music, as it helps with reverencing the moment. Remind the participants that they can return to their imagination at any time and be with

Jesus in this very real way. Encourage them to place their art expression in their home to remind them that Jesus' invitation requires a response and that salvation is the Lord's gift to them.

CLOSING For closure to the meditation experience, have different participants lead the following litany of blessing:

> *Litany Response*
> Blessed be the Lord of Salvation.
>
> Thank you, Lord, for your invitation to hurry and come down. [All respond.]
> Praise to you, Lord, for your acceptance of me, a sinner. [All respond.]
> Thank you, Lord, for your listening presence at table. [All respond.]
> Praise to you, Lord, for your gift of saving grace. [All respond.]
> Thank you, Lord, for your compassion and peace. [All respond.]
> Praise to you, Lord, for your gentle blessing. [All respond.]
> Thank you, Lord, for your constant fidelity as we strive to recreate our lives in response to your invitation. [All respond.]
>
> [Additional prayers may be added at this time.]
>
> Lord, because of your great love for us, you have called us by name and have saved us. Grant us the courage to come down from the tree whenever we need to and share those things that burden us. With your saving grace, help us to be faithful to our new commitment to positive, concrete actions in our life, and allow us to call others down from their tree and bring them into a trusting relationship with you. Amen.

Joy
I Am Chosen, Too!

This affirming prayer experience, "I Am Chosen, Too!" is based on Mary's magnificat. The same joy can be ours if we open ourselves to the awareness that God "has done great things" for us and through us and that ours must be a willing and resounding "yes!" each time we are chosen.

THEME After you have given directions to the participants and set the tone for meditation, introduce the theme by saying something like the following:

> It is necessary to take inventory of our life and to acknowledge with joy the ways we have been chosen by Yahweh. Mary's magnificat reminds us we must proclaim that our God has done great things for us and through us and that we must be open time and again to yet another "yes" asked of us as we follow Jesus, her

Son. . . . The joy comes in knowing that it is Yahweh who seeks us out and chooses us over and over again!

OPENING   Read aloud this opening prayer:

Hail Mary, Blessed Mary, you who have named your experiences as gifts from the Most High, grace us with your gentle presence that we might come to the deeper awareness that God has done great things for us and through us. Guide us into the sanctuary of our heart that we might recognize the many "yeses" in our lives that we have already given to your Son. Help us also to discover the "yeses" that we still must speak . . . and to share any obstacles that might make us hesitant in our commitment to the same Lord in whom you believed. Allow this to be a time of great joy for us as we come to realize that, like you, we are chosen, too! We ask all this through the intercession of your holy name, Mary. Amen.

SCRIPTURE   Read aloud Luke 1:39–56, using a Bible.

SCRIPT   Play the "I Am Chosen, Too!" meditation on the accompanying recording or slowly and reverently read aloud the following script for the guided meditation. Play soft, instrumental background music.

Today you will enter the hush of your quiet place and meet Mary in your imagination. First, you will begin by doing some deep-breathing exercises. When I say to, if you can, breathe in and out through your nose very quietly during these exercises. Close your eyes and get comfortable. You will be relaxing your entire body.

Breathe in deeply . . . hold it . . . breathe out slowly and completely. Breathe in deeply . . . hold it . . . breathe out slowly and completely. Again, breathe in deeply . . . hold it . . . breathe out slowly and completely.

Allow your feet and ankles to relax. Relax your legs and your hips. Stay mindful of your breathing. Relax your stomach muscles, and now your chest. . . . Just relax. Let your arms grow limp. . . . Relax your wrists, your hands, and your fingers. . . . Keep breathing in deeply and out slowly.

Allow your shoulders to become heavy. . . . Let all the tension drain from your shoulders. . . . Relax your neck, your facial muscles, and even your eyelids. . . . Just relax. . . . Breathe in deeply . . . hold it . . . breathe out slowly and completely. [Pause.]

You are sitting in your favorite room. There is a sense of peace here because you are all alone; it is a room you have made your own. Look around you . . . discover what makes it special. . . . It is a place where you can return to God some of the talents and gifts that were given to you at your birth.

As you sit here, remember one person whom you have touched this year. . . . You think about how you might have helped or comforted this person. You reflect on the ways you made a difference in this person's life.

A knock at the door interrupts your thinking. You go to the door and open it. . . . It is Mary . . . the mother of Jesus. . . . See the warmth in her smile as she greets you by name and tells you that she is glad to find you here alone. . . .

Notice how you are feeling to have Mary, the greatest of all disciples, come to see you.

Invite her to sit down. . . . She seems very comfortable to be in your room with you. Watch her face as she leans in toward you to talk with you.

Listen as she tells you that she is here to thank you for your "yes" to her Son . . . for your following Jesus . . . for your bringing others, young and old, closer to him. Hear her name one of your "yeses" that has been pleasing to Yahweh. . . .

Hear her name some of the people that you have influenced by your caring and concern. . . . She names people about whom you have even forgotten. . . . Notice how you are feeling to be appreciated by Mary, Most Holy.

Feel her gentle hands as she takes your hands. Mary asks you now to name an area of hurt or frustration that she can help you with . . . that she can give her Son to hold with her. . . .

Listen as she tells you that she wants nothing to be an obstacle in your following her Son . . . that she desires a very real place for you. Spend this time talking with Mary and allowing her into the very sanctuary of your heart. Hear her respond to what troubles you. . . .

Listen now as she tells you of the ways that you have grown . . . in your personal life or spiritual life. . . . Allow yourself to feel joy to be so acknowledged.

She now tells you of the great joy that has been hers to have been chosen by Yahweh. She shares with you where her "yes" has taken her . . . through happy moments and through sorrowful ones.

Listen as she speaks. . . . She tells you that your life is not unlike hers . . . and that Yahweh's love is constant through the calm that enfolds you and through the storms that shake you. Hear her remind you to call on the power of the Spirit and the presence of her Son daily . . . and to rejoice in the Almighty who has done great things for you.

Hear yourself respond to Mary. . . . Is there another or deeper "yes" that you can commit to in your relationship with the Lord? Name it now for Mary.

It is time for Mary to go now. . . . She holds your face between her hands. . . . Once more she whispers, "Thank you" . . . as she looks at you with love.

Express in some way how you are feeling, and then say your good-byes. . . . You accompany Mary to the door and watch her as she walks away. . . . She turns one more time to look at and wave to you. . . . Return to where you were sitting and allow yourself to experience the joy of your visit . . . the joy of being chosen, like Mary, to follow her Son.

Breathe in deeply . . . hold it . . . breathe out slowly and completely. Breathe in deeply . . . hold it . . . breathe out slowly and completely. Once more, breathe in deeply . . . hold it . . . breathe out slowly and completely. And when you are ready, you may open your eyes.

REFLECTION Continue to play instrumental music. Ask the participants to reflect on the experience that they have just gone through by pondering some of the following questions. You might want to suggest that they respond to those questions that speak most to them. Allow time for them to write their reflections.

- What was the room in which I found myself? What was special about it?
- What are the talents or gifts that I have been given since birth?
- Whom did I name as a person I have touched this year?
- How did I feel having Mary come to visit me in my favorite room?

- What was a "yes" in my life that was pleasing to Yahweh and for which Mary thanked me?
- What emotions were evoked when Mary thanked me and began naming more persons whom I have influenced by my caring and concern? Whom did Mary name that I had forgotten?
- What did I share with Mary as something that she and her Son could help hold for me? Did I feel better for having shared it with her?
- What did Mary name as ways that I have grown in my personal or spiritual life? Could I feel joy to be so acknowledged by Mary?
- What did Mary tell me of her own joys or sorrows that I will especially remember from her sharing with me?
- Describe what I named for Mary as another or deeper "yes" that I can commit to in my relationship with the Lord.
- Could I let myself feel Mary's love and gratitude toward me? If so, why? If not, why not?
- How did I express myself when I said good-bye to Mary?
- Can I claim joy for being chosen, too? If so, why? If not, why not?
- What is the most special message or image that I will take away with me from this prayer experience?

ART EXPRESSION AND PRAYER RITUAL (OPTIONAL)

The art expression is an optional activity. It can be used in place of the reflection questions. If you decide to use this activity, prepare the art area before the group gathers. At each place, have glue or glue sticks, construction or tissue paper of various colors, and a piece of white art paper or small white poster board.

After the meditation, continue playing quiet instrumental music in the art area. Invite the group to move to one of the prepared places. Direct the participants to make a mosaic of colors that will express what they have just gone through in their prayer experience.

The participants are to tear pieces off the various colored construction or tissue papers and design their mosaic on the white art paper or poster board. The pieces they tear off can be as big or as small as they choose. Their mosaic can be made into a shape, symbol, a word or words, or it can become an abstract design or splash of colors. Remind the participants that the colors that they use should speak of their prayer experience.

If anyone needs help, you could explain that colors can represent the room where they met Mary, the people whom they have touched, the "yes" in their lives that has been pleasing to God, the troubled area they shared with Mary, the "yes" that they still need to make, the feelings they had throughout the experience, and the like.

Explain that sharing faith experiences can help strengthen one another's faith. Then invite the participants to share their prayer experiences by explaining the parts of their mosaic that they feel comfortable sharing. Add the instruction that when everyone is finished sharing, each participant is to place their artwork in the prayer center—overlapping the one of the previous person, to create one big mosaic as a prayer offering.

Allow enough time for the sharing and affirming of each person. Continue playing instrumental music, as it helps with reverencing the moment. Remind the participants that they can return to their imagination at any time and be with Mary in this very real way. Encourage them to place their art expression in their favorite room or somewhere in their home to remind them of their time with Mary and the wonderful joy that is theirs because they are chosen, too! God has done great things for them and through them!

CLOSING   For closure to the meditation experience, read aloud the following prayer:

> Blessed Mary . . . holy, gentle woman of God, thank you for your affirmation of us as we strive to follow your example of discipleship . . . of saying "yes" time and again to Yahweh, who chooses us with the same

sincerity as when you were chosen. Continue to grace our life with knowing moments in which we can reach out, touch others, and affect change. Grant us healing in the areas that inhibit our saying "yes" with full commitment to your Son. Pray for us that we might continue to grow in our personal and spiritual lives and become even more pleasing to the Most High. Finally, lead us in ways that we will experience the wonderful joy of acknowledging that God has done great things for us, as well as the incredible joy of knowing that like you, Mary, we have been chosen, too! This is our prayer that we now lift up to you through the power of your Son, Jesus. Amen.

Faith
Walking on Water

This prayer experience, "Walking on Water," invites us to a faith centered in trust—the same kind of faith needed when the Lord invited Peter to come, walk on the water.

THEME   After you have given directions to the participants and set the tone for meditation, introduce the theme by saying something like the following:

> There is a certain amount of trust that must be mine if I am to make the great strides of which I am capable. The Lord who calls to Peter to walk upon the water is the same Lord who calls me to risk meeting him across the waves of my own life. I have only to stay . . . in the hush of my quiet place.

OPENING Read aloud this opening prayer:

> Lord, you who call me to great faith, be present with me now so that I may hear you speak the words that will urge me to move mountains. Help me to walk upon the water and to place my fears in your hands. Amen.

SCRIPTURE Read aloud Matthew 14:15–33, using a Bible.

SCRIPT Play the "Walking on Water" meditation on the accompanying recording or slowly and reverently read aloud the following script for the guided meditation. Play soft, instrumental background music.

> Today you will enter the hush of your quiet place and meet Jesus in your imagination. First, you will begin by doing some deep-breathing exercises. When I say to, if you can, breathe in and out through your nose very quietly during these exercises. Close your eyes and get comfortable. You will be relaxing your entire body.
>
> Breathe in deeply . . . hold it . . . breathe out slowly and completely. Breathe in deeply . . . hold it . . . breathe out slowly and completely. Again, breathe in deeply . . . hold it . . . breathe out slowly and completely.
>
> Allow your feet and ankles to relax. Relax your legs and your hips. Stay mindful of your breathing. Relax your stomach muscles, and now your chest. . . . Just relax. Let your arms grow limp. . . . Relax your wrists, your hands, and your fingers. . . . Keep breathing in deeply and out slowly.
>
> Allow your shoulders to become heavy. . . . Let all the tension drain from your shoulders. . . .

Relax your neck, your facial muscles, and even your eyelids. . . . Just relax. . . . Breathe in deeply . . . hold it . . . breathe out slowly and completely. [Pause.]

It is after three o'clock in the morning, and you are sitting by moonlight in the boat with the twelve Apostles. No one seems tired because they are discussing yesterday's miracle performed by Jesus. . . . The sea is somewhat rough, but the discussion is so lively that at first no one is taking notice of it. Thomas is saying if he hadn't seen the multiplication of the five loaves and the two fish with his own eyes, he wouldn't believe it. John speaks next. You turn to watch the expression on this young man's face when he proclaims with loving conviction that Jesus is truly his Lord. . . . Peter, who is standing and holding loosely to some rigging, is shaking his head in amazement while saying, "And imagine! Twelve baskets were left over!" Without warning, a gigantic wave slaps at the boat, Peter almost loses his footing, but Matthew grabs him, and a few of the Apostles move to secure the lines of rope and the attached nets. There is a definite smell in the air announcing an imminently approaching storm.

The sea is becoming rougher, whitecaps sit angrily on the waves, and the sky is growing darker. . . . You watch as huge, gray, threatening clouds move in to obscure the moonlight. The wind has picked up and begins to fling stinging saltwater on your face. . . . The discussion of the miracle is dropped and the concerns about the weather are beginning to be voiced. . . . Your nervousness and that of the others builds up around you.

The swells of the waves continue to grow higher and stronger. They look like mighty dragons burrowing forward and ferociously raising their ugly heads. You are soaking wet from the saltwater that has crashed over and into the boat. Your craft seems so small as it is carelessly tossed about. . . . Almost everyone is working to keep the boat under control and from tipping over. Others are merely trying to hold onto the wooden sides of the boat.

Suddenly, a couple of the disciples are wildly leaning into the face of a wave and gesturing crazily. You move with the others to try to see what they are pointing to. Finally, you understand the words, "It's a ghost!" Like the waves, fear seems to drench everyone.

A familiar voice carries over the wind. . . . "Courage, my friends . . . it is I! Do not be so foolish as to be afraid." The Apostles are murmuring, "Is it Jesus? Can it be the Lord? Look, he walks upon the water!"

You watch Peter cry out and you, too, are drawn to the figure approaching on the water. You are filled with a desire to believe unwaveringly in him. You hunger to meet him. Hear yourself call out, "Lord, if it is really you, tell me to come to you." Above the roar of the waves and the wind, hear Jesus call you by name to come and to walk on the water to him.

You climb out of the boat with James and John, each holding one of your arms to lower you. . . . You turn to Jesus and begin to walk on the water toward him. . . . Notice how you are feeling to be walking on water. The waves slap at your ankles and curl around behind you, but you do not sink. You must even walk headlong into the wind to get to him . . . but you do not sink.

Jesus is only five feet away now, and you can see the encouragement he gives you with the grin on his face. You continue to put one foot in front of the other . . . almost ready to reach him. Unexpectedly, a gale of wind knocks into you and you are frightened by it . . . and perhaps you are frightened of even more than the wind because you begin to sink. What fears, despairs, and self-doubt cause you to falter? Is it too much to believe that you can walk on water, even though it is Jesus who invited you to do so? Hear yourself cry out, "Lord, please save me!"

Two strong hands grab hold of you and pull you back up. . . . Hear Jesus say, "You have so little faith . . . why did you doubt? Believe in me." Allow yourself to trust that this Jesus will not let you drown. . . . Take the last two steps to bring you closer to Jesus. Jesus grabs you to him in delight. You hear his laughter in your ear. It startles you, but it is a laughter that says, "Hooray! You did it!" Allow yourself to start laughing, too! Enjoy this moment of triumph with Jesus.

Jesus now turns you to head you back to the boat. . . . Just once you look over your shoulder to make sure that he is following you. . . . He is. James and John are ready to hoist you into the boat. Peter and Thomas help Jesus in. At once, you notice the wind drops down and the waves become calm.

Everyone starts talking at once, but Jesus quiets them. Listen as he tells them that they are safe now and to go to sleep. . . . But not you; . . . he takes you by the hand and leads you into a corner of the boat where the others are not settling down. . . . Jesus wraps a blanket around your shoulders as you sit together. . . . Listen as Jesus invites you to share your fears, your despairs, your self-doubts, or anything that makes your faith in him waver. Take this time to tell Jesus all that is in your heart. Listen carefully to the responses that he gives you as you talk together. . . .

Jesus reminds you that he believes in you and he asks you to have greater trust and faith in him. . . . He places his warm hands over yours, which are wrapped in the blanket. . . . Hear him as he wishes you peace and a night of rest. . . . He tells you that you will face tomorrow differently because you are able to believe in him more deeply as your Lord. . . . Can you feel the confidence that Jesus places in you? Hear Jesus whisper your name and that he loves you. . . . Express what you yourself are feeling and say your good night to Jesus in whatever way is comfortable for you. . . .

Snuggle down and allow yourself to become very restful as you listen to the gentle lapping of the waves against the hull. Quietly you recall the events of this night and, gratefully, you remember the profound sharing you had with Jesus.

Breathe in deeply . . . hold it . . . breathe out slowly and completely. Breathe in deeply . . . hold it . . . breathe out slowly and completely. Once more, breathe in deeply . . . hold it . . . breathe out slowly and completely. And when you are ready, you may open your eyes.

REFLECTION   Continue to play instrumental music. Ask the participants to reflect on the experience that they have just gone through by pondering some of the following questions. You might want to suggest that they respond to those questions that speak most to them. Allow time for them to write their reflections.

- What did it feel like to be in the boat with the twelve Apostles at three o'clock in the morning?
- Did I have any particular viewpoint or feeling regarding the miracle of the loaves and fish that the Apostles were talking about?
- What did it feel like to be in the midst of a storm? Have I had similar feelings before? If so, when?
- What emotions was I feeling when I called out to Jesus to prove that it was he by telling me to come to him across the water?
- How did I feel when Jesus called me by name to come to him?
- What doubts and fears caused me to falter?
- Did I trust that Jesus would save me? Why? Why not?
- Was I surprised by Jesus laughing in delight when he finally caught hold of me? What did his laughter mean to me?
- Why was it important for me to look back and make sure that Jesus was following me to the boat?
- What was my reaction when I noticed that the wind and waves had died down once Jesus and I got into the boat?
- How did I feel when Jesus told everyone else to go to sleep but wanted to spend time with me?
- When Jesus placed the blanket around my shoulders, what was I thinking or feeling?
- What was the most important concern that I got off my chest during my sharing with Jesus? What was Jesus' response?
- Has my faith and trust in Jesus deepened at all because of this prayer experience?
- Could I truly feel his words when Jesus said he loved me?
- How did I express myself to him and say good night?
- What is the most special message or image that I will remember from this prayer experience?

ART EXPRESSION AND PRAYER RITUAL (OPTIONAL)

The art expression is an optional activity. It can be used in place of the reflection questions. If you decide to use this activity, prepare the art area before the group gathers. At each place, have crayons or watercolor paints and brushes, white or manila drawing paper, cups of water and paper toweling (if painting is to be done), and clay or play dough (optional).

After the meditation, continue playing quiet music in the art area. Invite the participants to move to one of the prepared places. Direct them to sketch a boat in the middle of their paper, or to mold one out of clay or play dough, if provided. Encourage them to use colors to symbolize their personal storm of fears, self-doubts, and the like, that make their faith falter. Have them express the effect their time with Jesus had on them. If the boat is drawn or painted, direct the participants to make sketches around the craft as well. If the boat is three-dimensional, have the participants place it on the paper when they are done sculpting it.

Explain that sharing faith experiences can help strengthen one another's faith. Then invite the participants to take turns sharing the symbolism of the colors they used and the boat they created. Add that when they have done this, they are all to place their boats in the center of the table as a sign of the support they will offer one another through storms and calm alike.

Allow enough time for the sharing and affirming of each person. Continue playing instrumental music, as it helps with reverencing the moment. Remind the participants that they can return to their imagination at any time and be with Jesus in this very real way. Encourage them to place their art expression in their home to remind them that Jesus calmly exists in the midst of their storms—that he gladly calls to them to come, walk on water—while asking at the same time that their faith, rooted in trust, deepen in him.

CLOSING   For closure to the meditation experience, read aloud the following prayer:

> Lord Jesus, you walk amid the storms of our life that is filled with doubt, despair, and fears. . . . You lean across the water to save us when we begin to sink. . . . You are steadfast in your caring of us and in your belief in us. Thank you, once again, for sharing the reality of this during our prayer and sharing time today. Be present in us and around us as we struggle to become people with deeper faith and trust in you. Help us always to call to you across the ferocious winds and waves of our daily experiences that we might find the calm and quiet in you that we need. Give us the guidance to be able to quell threatening storms for one another by leading our sisters and brothers to you across so many troubled waters. With confidence, we place our belief in you as we lift up this prayer in your name. Amen.

Healing
Time to Unbend

This healing prayer experience, "Time to Unbend," is based on the story of the crippled woman who was bent over for eighteen years and healed by Jesus on the Sabbath. It reminds us that Jesus also calls us to unbend and to rid our life of whatever keeps us from standing tall.

THEME After you have given directions to the participants and set the tone for meditation, introduce the theme by saying something like the following:

> It is good to enter a place within to be quiet and self-reflective—to examine the things, events, or people in our lives that we allow to cripple us—that we allow to keep us bent over—that we allow to keep us from standing tall. Jesus will be there for us and risk with us in our pain just as he did for the crippled woman.

OPENING   Read aloud this opening prayer:

> You who are holy, breathe into us the spirit of self-love, courage, and forgiveness as we quiet ourselves in readiness to spend time with you. We pray with hope that we can honestly face with you those people, situations, or things that bend us over. Help us to trust that you will bring us to healing, peace, and empowerment. Be with us now in the hush of our quiet place. Amen.

SCRIPTURE   Read aloud Luke 13:10–17, using a Bible.

SCRIPT   Play the "Time to Unbend" meditation on the accompanying recording or slowly and reverently read aloud the following script for the guided meditation. Play soft, instrumental background music.

> Today you will enter the hush of your quiet place and meet Jesus in your imagination. First, you will begin by doing some deep-breathing exercises. When I say to, if you can, breathe in and out through your nose very quietly during these exercises. Close your eyes and get comfortable. You will be relaxing your entire body.
>
> Breathe in deeply . . . hold it . . . breathe out slowly and completely. Breathe in deeply . . . hold it . . . breathe out slowly and completely. Again, breathe in deeply . . . hold it . . . breathe out slowly and completely.
>
> Allow your feet and ankles to relax. Relax your legs and your hips. Stay mindful of your breathing. Relax your stomach muscles, and now your chest. . . . Just relax. Let your arms grow limp. . . . Relax your wrists, your hands, and your fingers. . . . Keep breathing in deeply and out slowly.

Allow your shoulders to become heavy. . . .
Let all the tension drain from your shoulders. . . .
Relax your neck, your facial muscles, and even your
eyelids. . . . Just relax. . . . Breathe in deeply . . .
hold it . . . breathe out slowly and completely.
[Pause.]

You are in the crowd that has gathered in
the synagogue to hear Jesus teach, and he has just
finished his last message. You watch Jesus as he
looks around at all the people. . . . He seems to be
taking in everyone with his kind, compassionate
eyes. . . . They stop and rest on a woman who has
struggled the entire time to look at him from her
bent form. Her shoulders are misshapen and her
head is barely at an angle where her eyes can look
up to see him. Hear Jesus call her to him. . . . Her
face is doubtful; it asks, "Is he calling me?" People
urge her forward. You watch her as she approaches
him, her crooked body, slowly, painfully shuffling
through the crowd. . . . She stops before Jesus,
who places one hand on her humped shoulders,
. . . with the other he cradles her chin. She strains
to look at him. Her face is expectant and hopeful
and disbelieving that she has been chosen.

"Woman," Jesus speaks. His voice is warm,
tender, and strong. "You are freed from your dis-
ability." You watch as the hand on her shoulder
strokes her back. . . . The hand beneath her chin
aids her to straighten her head and neck. . . . It
catches the tears that are streaming down her
cheeks. . . . Perhaps she cries because her muscles
have moved for the first time, yawning from their
slumber of eighteen years, and her bones from their
inertia. . . . You know it is painful sometimes to
move through to newness. . . . She does not

recognize herself; it is almost too much! You watch as Jesus continues to talk quietly to her. She is fully alive now! She is standing tall! She believes! She begins to glorify her God, and her prayer seems to dance in the air!

People all around you are shouting in amazement and in thanksgiving. Notice what your reaction is to have witnessed this.

Suddenly, the president of the synagogue begins to criticize Jesus for healing on the Sabbath. You listen to the argument. Jesus is firm in his reply: "Hypocrites, you would untie your animals to water them on the Sabbath. Doesn't this woman deserve to be freed after eighteen years?"

The crowd cheers, and his enemies are left confused at another law Jesus has challenged. You see them walk away muttering.

Jesus lovingly scans the crowd once again, and his eyes rest on you. Hear him call you by name. . . . Notice how you are feeling as you weave yourself through the crowd. . . . You stand before Jesus, who places an arm about your shoulders. He leans in toward you to whisper an invitation to walk with him.

As you leave the noisy synagogue behind, hear Jesus gently ask you, "Tell me what keeps you bent over, what cripples you." Hear him say, "Tell me everything. Tell me anything."

Take this time now to share with Jesus as you walk through town and then along the shore. . . .

Hear Jesus challenge you to name what will free you, what it is that will help you to unbend. . . .

Listen as he responds to what you have said. . . .

As you continue walking, you near some rocks. You and Jesus sit comfortably. Jesus takes both of your hands in his. Hear him thank you for all those whom you have helped to unbend. Listen as Jesus gratefully names the people whom you have touched. Powerfully, together, you pray for their lives. . . . Jesus reminds you that in your help to unbend them you have become less crippled each time.

Jesus asks you now to name those who have helped you to stand tall. . . . Together you lift them up in a prayer of thanksgiving.

Now Jesus just looks at you . . . quietly and deeply. Feel this warmth as he places his hands upon your head; . . . allow yourself to feel his power and love course through you. Listen while he prays just for you. . . . You will never forget this prayer.

It is time to leave each other. Is there a part of you that no longer feels doubled over? Do you stand taller, straighter? You take a moment to express to each other what this time together has meant.

As you begin your good-byes, hear Jesus assure you that he will be with you always. Allow yourself to believe in these words.

Hear the sincerity in his voice as he says your name and "I love you." Listen as he reminds you of one thing. . . . What does he tell you? Will you promise to remember it? Hear yourself respond to Jesus.

Share a final good-bye. Watch now as Jesus returns to the synagogue—toward others who need him. You know you stand taller, straighter, stronger as you watch him disappear after a last wave to you.

Breathe in deeply . . . hold it . . . breathe out slowly and completely. Breathe in deeply . . . hold it . . . breathe out slowly and completely. Once more, breathe in deeply . . . hold it . . . breathe out slowly and completely. And when you are ready, you may open your eyes.

REFLECTION

Continue to play instrumental music. Ask the participants to reflect on the experience that they have just gone through by pondering some of the following questions. You might want to suggest that they respond to those questions that speak most to them. Allow time for them to write their reflections.

- How did I feel to see Jesus heal the woman who was bent over?
- What did I share with Jesus about what keeps me bent over?
- What did I share with Jesus that makes me stand taller?
- Whom did Jesus name that I helped to unbend?
- Whom did I name as the persons who have helped me to unbend?
- What was Jesus' prayer for me? Could I feel myself becoming straighter and stronger?
- What decisions have I made and what insights have I come to as a result of my time with Jesus?
- Did I allow myself to feel Jesus' warm hands in blessing upon my head? Did Jesus and I share any other expression of affection? How did this (these) make me feel?
- What was the one thing that Jesus reminded me of before leaving? Will I remember it?
- What is the most special message or image that I will remember from this prayer experience?

ART EXPRESSION AND PRAYER RITUAL (OPTIONAL)

The art expression is an optional activity. It can be used in place of the reflection questions. If you decide to use this activity, prepare the art area before the group gathers. At each place, have crayons or watercolor paints and brushes, white or manila drawing paper, and cups of water and paper toweling (if painting is to be done).

After the meditation, continue playing quiet music in the art area. Invite the participants to move to one of the prepared places. Direct them to express, on half of the paper, what keeps them bent over. They can use colors, symbols, or words to do this. Instruct them to use the other half of the paper to express what will help them to stand taller and stronger.

Explain that sharing faith experiences can help strengthen one another's faith. Then invite them to share the effect the prayer time had on them by explaining the colors and symbols on their artwork. Add that after they have finished explaining, they are to fold under the part of the paper showing that which bends them over and place faceup the side of the paper showing that which helps them to unbend. These are to be placed in the middle of the prayer circle.

Allow time for the sharing and affirming of each person. Continue playing instrumental music, as it helps with reverencing the moment. Remind the participants that they can return to their imagination at any time and be with Jesus in this very real way. Encourage them to place their art expression in their home to remind them that Jesus calls them to unbend and stand tall.

CLOSING
For closure to the meditation experience, lead the following thanksgiving litany:

> *Litany response*
> Thank you, you who are holy, heal us to stand tall.
>
> *Leader*
> For the people in our lives who believe in us and help us to unbend. [All respond.]
>
> *Leader*
> For your limitless presence and forgiveness that frees us of our disabilities. [All respond.]

Leader

For the events in our life that invite us to grow and to
reach out in empathy to help others to straighten.
[All respond.]

Leader

For the things that bind us . . . the compulsive behav-
iors, substance abuse, self-doubt, fears, relationships, and jobs . . . that we may victoriously win
over them and no longer be crippled. [All respond.]

Leader

For finding you in the quiet here and for entering into
deeper intimacy with you. [All respond.]

Leader

For the courage, the grace, and the empowerment to
hold on to that which unbends us. [All respond.]

ACKNOWLEDGMENTS
(continued)

With all my love and gratitude, I thank Aggie, whose personal belief in and helpful support of me has made it possible to complete this third manuscript peacefully in the midst of organized chaos.

To Fr. Robert Stamschror, my editor, whose affirmation is unceasing, and to the publishing team for this book, I express my gratefulness for another work brought to fruition.

Sincere and loving appreciation must be expressed to my sister, Cheryl, for the hours spent typing and for the gentle moments of feedback given over quiet cups of shared coffee and tea during sunrises on her porch.

To Barry Russo, whose giftedness has yet again provided the moving background music on synthesizer for these meditations, I am indebted.

For the painless and oftentimes humorous experiences of recording afforded me by Anthony "Barrel" Marrapese of Reel to Real Recording Studio, Cranston, Rhode Island, I give thanks.

And to those who have and continue to provide me with experiences of the Holy: Isabel, Shirley, Jean, Eileen, Alycia, Sr. Mary George, Pauline, Jon, CWC, Fr. Jude, Aunt Mary, B. J., Bob, Lisa, Sue, Kathy, Libby, Belle, my community at Saint Cecilia's School, the Community of Saint Benedict in New Jersey, those who have hired me for retreat work, and my Mom and Dad; you are truly blessings, and I love you.

Other Guided Meditations
available from Saint Mary's Press

Guided Meditations for Youth on Personal Themes

Jane E. Arsenault

These meditations on discipleship, new life, secrets, and self-esteem can be used by youth ministers, catechists, teachers, and liturgists in a variety of settings. The leader's guide contains directions for preparing for the meditations, the meditation scripts, and directions for follow-up. The audiocassette contains high-quality recordings of the meditation scripts against a background of original music.

Leader's guide: ISBN 0-88489-347-2
7½ x 9¼, 47 pages, stitched, $8.95

Audiocassette: ISBN 0-88489-354-5
90 minutes, $7.95

Guided Meditations for Youth on Sacramental Life

Jane E. Arsenault and Jean R. Cedor

The format of these guided meditations on baptism, the Eucharist, and confirmation includes both a leader's guide and an audiocassette. The leader's guide contains directions for preparing for the meditations, the meditation scripts, and suggestions for follow-up after the meditations. The audiocassette contains high-quality recordings of the meditation scripts with original background music. These meditations can be used with young people in a variety of settings.

Leader's guide: ISBN 0-88489-308-1
7½ x 9¼, 40 pages, stitched, $8.95

Audiocassette: ISBN 0-88489-309-X
90 minutes, $7.95

"Jane presented her guided meditation, 'I Am Chosen, Too!' for our sixty-five faculty and staff at our annual retreat. It was a very moving experience in prayer that helped all of us become more aware of God's presence in ourselves and each other."

Bruce R. Daigle, Administrator, Greater Woonsocket Catholic Regional School System, Woonsocket, RI

"Our faculty retreat was a positive experience because of Jane's guided prayer, 'Time to Unbend.' Her meditation stirred the hearts of twenty-four faculty members to share as never before."

Martha Mulligan, RSM, Mercymount Country Day School, Cumberland, RI